AMAZING SCIENCE
PLANTS

Sally Hewitt

WAYLAND

Published in paperback in 2014 by Wayland
Copyright © 2014 Wayland

Hachette Children's Books
338 Euston Road, London NW1 3BH

Senior Editor: Joyce Bentley
Senior Design Manager: Rosamund Saunders
Designer: Tall Tree

British Library Cataloguing in Publication Data
Hewitt, Sally
        Plants. - (Amazing Science)
        1. Botany - Juvenile literature
        2. Plants - Juvenile literature
        I. Title
        580

ISBN-13: 978-0-7502-8060-0

Printed and bound in China

10 9 8 7 6 5 4 3 2 1

Wayland is a division of Hachette Children's Books, an Hachette UK Company.
www.hachette.co.uk

Cover: A sunflower (Photographers Choice/Getty Images)
Title page: Wasp on a flower (Corbis)

Corbis: 2, 10, 11, 15. Mode Images/Photo Library: 6.
Bsip/Photo Library: 7. Mark Hamblin/Photo Library: 8.
Christopher Talbot Frank/Photo Library: 9. Andrew
Brown/Ecoscene: 12. Iconica/Getty Images: 13. David
Wootton/Ecoscene: 14. Photonica/Getty Images: 16, 17, 27.
Photographers Choice/Getty Images: 18. Sally
Morgan/Ecoscene: 19. Stone/Getty Images: 20. Nick
Hawkes/Ecoscene: 21. First Light/Getty Images: 22.
Taxi/Getty Images: 23, 24. Kjell Sandved/Ecoscene: 25. Paul
Edmondson/Corbis: 26.

Contents

Amazing plants

Giant sequoia trees are the tallest plants on Earth. They grow to over 90 metres tall and can weigh 2,000 tonnes.

Plants are alive. They need air, light and water to live and grow.

A plant can be as big as a tree or as small as a daisy.

A daisy is a kind of plant that grows flowers.

YOUR TURN!

You are alive. Plants are alive. What other things are alive?

SCIENCE WORDS: alive grow plant

Where do plants grow?

Plants grow everywhere from mountains to under the sea. All kinds of plants can grow in one small wood.

Plants find ways of growing wherever they can find air, light and water.

Cactus plants grow in deserts where there is plenty of light but very little water.

YOUR TURN!

Find an area of a park or garden. How many different plants can you find growing around you?

A cactus stores water in its thick stem when it rains.

SCIENCE WORDS: **air   light   water**

Parts of a plant

Most parts of a plant grow above ground but roots grow under the soil. They can be the biggest part of a plant.

Every part of a plant does an important job. Roots suck up water.

The stem supports the plant. Green leaves make food and flowers are where new seeds are made.

YOUR TURN!

Pull up a weed and look carefully at the parts.

flower

This amaryllis is a kind of plant that grows flowers.

stem

leaf

roots

SCIENCE WORDS: flower leaf roots stem

Sunlight

In the rainforest smaller plants grow high up on the branches of trees so they can be nearer the light.

Plants use energy from sunlight to make food in their green leaves.

Some trees store food in the summer. They lose their leaves in winter as there is less sunlight.

YOUR TURN!

Put a pot plant in a dark place for several days. What happens to it?

Some green leaves turn red and gold in autumn before they die in winter.

SCIENCE WORDS: **food   sunlight**

Flowers

The rafflesia from South East Asia is the biggest flower in the world. Flies visit it because of its rotten smell.

Flowers are the part of a plant where seeds are made.

Flowers use a dust called pollen to make seeds. Pollen sticks to an insect when it visits the flower for food.

YOUR TURN!

On a sunny day, watch insects visit flowers for food. Look for pollen sticking to their legs and bodies.

Insects carry pollen from flower to flower so new seeds can be made.

SCIENCE WORDS: insect pollen seed

Fruit and seeds

A watermelon has pink juicy flesh and black seeds. It is the part of a plant called the fruit. It is yummy to eat!

When a flower dies, the fruit grows and falls. Fruit gives seeds the food they need to grow into a new plant.

Nuts are seeds. Squirrels eat some nuts and bury others in the ground to eat later.

YOUR TURN!

Ask an adult to help you cut open some fruit. Find the seeds inside.

Some of the buried nuts grow into trees.

SCIENCE WORDS: fruit   nut

17

Seedlings

A tall sunflower grows from a little stripy seed. Inside the seed is everything it needs to grow.

A seed grows into a new plant called a seedling.

The seedling grows into a plant that makes new seeds and the life cycle starts again.

YOUR TURN!

Plant a bean in a jam jar lined with kitchen towels. Keep the towels damp and watch your bean grow into a seedling.

SCIENCE WORDS: **life cycle seedling shoot**

Plants to eat

Fields of golden wheat stretch as far as the eye can see. Wheat is a grass. It is one of the many plants we can eat.

Wheat seeds, called grain, are ground into flour to make bread and pasta.

We eat every part of a plant. Carrots are roots. Celery is a stem. Lettuces are leaves and broccoli is a flower.

The parts of a plant that we eat are called vegetables or fruit.

YOUR TURN!

What is your favourite vegetable? What part of a plant is it?

Useful plants

In some countries, trees are cut down for their wood. These logs are floating down river towards a saw mill.

Wood is cut at the mill then used to make furniture and paper.

Cotton for making clothes and rubber for making tyres also come from plants.

YOUR TURN!

Find things at home made from plants? What plants are they made from?

Medicine made from plants helps to make us better when we are ill.

SCIENCE WORDS: make wood

Extraordinary plants

A Venus flytrap needs air, water and light to grow, the same as other plants. But it eats animals too!

The Venus flytrap closes its leaves, like jaws, around a fly.

Plants called lithops pretend to be pebbles to protect themselves from hungry animals.

YOUR TURN!

What other ways do plants protect themselves from being eaten?

Lithops are hard to spot on pebbly ground.

Underwater plants

Underwater plants have long, bendy stems that sway in flowing water. Sea kelp clings tightly to the rocks.

Underwater plants need sunlight and oxygen to grow.

Bubbles of oxygen fill the water as the plants make food from sunlight.

YOUR TURN!

Look for plants that grow up walls and trees. Why do you think they have long bendy stems?

Underwater plants and animals all need oxygen to live and grow.

SCIENCE WORDS: oxygen underwater

Glossary

Air
An invisible gas that we need to live.

Alive
Things that are alive move, grow, eat and drink. A plant is alive and so are you.

Flower
The part of a plant where seeds are made.

Food
The things animals and plants take in for life and growth.

Fruit
The part of a plant that protects the seeds.

Grain
A grain is a small, hard seed.

Grow
To grow is to get bigger and change. A seed becomes a seedling, then a plant.

Insect
A small animal that has three pairs of legs, a body, a head and often wings.

Leaf
The part of a plant where the plant makes its food.

Life cycle
The growing stages of an animal or plant.

Light
Rays from the Sun, a torch or a lamp that allow us to see.

Make
To put things together. We make wooden furniture from tree trunks.

Nut
A nut is a kind of seed.

Oxygen
A gas in the air. Animals and plants need oxygen to live.

Plant
A living thing. It grows on the earth or in water and usually has green leaves.

Pollen
Yellow powder made by flowers.

Pretend
When something or someone looks or acts like something else.

Protect
To protect something is to stop it being harmed.

Root
The part of a plant that grows underground and sucks up water.

Seed
The part of a plant from which a new plant grows.

Seedling
A new, young plant.

Shoot
The part of a new young plant that grows up towards the light.

Stem
The part of a plant from where flowers and leaves grow.

Sunlight
Light from the sun. Plants make their food from sunlight.

Underwater
Underwater plants grow and live completely under water.

Water
A clear liquid that animals and plants take in for life and growth.

Wheat
A kind of grass. We make bread from grains of wheat.

Wood
Wood comes from a plant called a tree. We use it to make furniture and paper.

Index